# H.A.P.P.Y. B.I.R.T.H.D.A.Y.

*Happy Birthday: A Poem of Celebration*

ACRONYM POETRY GIFT SERIES

Copyright © 2021 by Macarena Luz Bianchi
MacarenaLuzB.com

Subscribe to the email list for this book spark.fyi/apc-hb

Zonia Iqbal, Illustrator neon.ly/ZoniaI

Imprint

Spark Social, Inc.
Miami, FL USA
SparkSocialPress.com

ISBN: Hardcover: 978-1-954489-14-1
Paperback: 978-1-954489-15-8
Ebook: 978-1-954489-16-5

Ordering Information: Special discounts are available on quantity purchases by corporations, associations, and others. For details, contact the publisher.

All rights reserved. No part of this book may be reproduced in any manner whatsoever without written permission except in the case of brief quotations embodied in critical articles and views. For permission requests, contact the publisher with subject: Excerpt Permissions.

# H.A.P.P.Y. B.I.R.T.H.D.A.Y.

## A Poem of Celebration

ACRONYM POETRY GIFT SERIES

Macarena Luz Bianchi

Imprint
Spark Social Press

How exquisite to be alive!

Acknowledge your lovely life.

Perseverance, no matter what.

Progress, always, with style and class.

You and your youthful heart,

        I appreciate you so much.

Beloved, you were born and blessed on this day.

It's time to celebrate
your special day.

# Radiate with playfulness, peace, and prosperity.

Thankful and connected
in every way, always.

Heartfelt humor, health, and harmony are yours.

Dare to dream what you wish to create this day, year, and beyond.

Accept all your gifts with
gratitude and grace.
You deserve to say, "Yes!"

You get more precious time
to live your glorious life filled
with laughter and full of fun.
May you have a Happy Birthday
from the bottom of my heart!

# H.A.P.P.Y. B.I.R.T.H.D.A.Y.
## A POEM OF CELEBRATION

How exquisite to be alive!

Acknowledge your glorious life.

Persevere, no matter what.

Progressing always with style and class.

You and your youthful heart are appreciated so much.


Born, beloved, and blessed on this day.

It's time to celebrate your special day.

Radiate with playfulness, peace, and prosperity.

Thankful and connected, in every way, always.

Heartfelt humor, health, and harmony are yours.

Dare to dream what you wish to create this day, year, and beyond.

Accept all your gifts with gratitude and grace. You deserve to say, "Yes!"

You get more precious time to live your glorious life filled with laughter

and full of fun. May you have a happy birthday from the bottom of my heart!

# Gift Book Series

## ACRONYM POETRY COLLECTION

- *Congratulations: A Poem of Triumph*
- *Friendship: A Poem of Appreciation*
- *Intimacy: A Poem of Adoration*
- *Anniversary: A Poem of Affection*
- *Sympathy: A Poem of Solace*
- *Valentine: A Poem of Love*

With more to come including: Encouragement, Graduation, and so on.

## POETRY COLLECTION

- *Glorious Mom: A Poem of Appreciation*
- *Gratitude Is: A Lighthearted Empowerment Poem*
- *Gratitude Is: Poem & Coloring Book*
- *The Grateful Giraffes: What is Gratitude?*

# About the Author

Macarena Luz Bianchi has a lighthearted and empowering approach and is affectionately considered a Fairy Godmother by her readers. She writes fiction and non-fiction for adults and children. She loves tea, flowers, and travel. Sign up for her newsletter and check out her other poems of appreciation, books, and more at MacarenaLuzB.com and subscribe to the email list for this book at spark.fyi/apc-hb.

www.ingramcontent.com/pod-product-compliance
Lightning Source LLC
Chambersburg PA
CBHW061108070526
44579CB00011B/180